# MURDER CON QUESO

*A Mexican Café Cozy Mystery*

## HOLLY PLUM

Copyright © 2017 by Holly Plum

All rights reserved. No part of this publication may be reproduced, stored in or introduced into a retrieval system, or transmitted, in any form, or by any means (electronic, mechanical, photocopying, recording, or otherwise) without the prior written permission of the copyright owner of this book.

This is a work of fiction. Names, characters, places, brands, media, and incidents are either the product of the author's imagination or are used fictitiously. Any resemblance to actual persons, living or dead, business establishments, events, or locales is entirely coincidental.

## CHAPTER ONE

Mari Ramirez could still remember a time not too long ago when she'd looked forward to moving back to her little hometown in southern Texas.

But her life had been very different back then.

Back then she had a tiring full-time teaching job, and she was still recovering from a nasty breakup with her *then* fiancé. On the night after she'd broken off her engagement, she'd called home to tell her mother what had happened. Her mother had simply told her to come home.

Because home was were Mari belonged.

*Home.* She hadn't expected the words to have such a profound effect on her. She'd spent so much of her youth trying to get away from the tiny town where she'd grown up, wanting to prove to her overbearing father that she could survive without him. Yet, she found herself back where she'd started working at her family's Mexican restaurant.

The most amusing part was that her teaching job now seemed like a piece of cake compared to the hurdles that came with running a small business, especially with family members for co-workers. Every evening after closing, Mari wanted nothing more than to climb into a warm bed and cocoon there for as long as she could. She enjoyed the long mornings on the back patio drinking mint tea with her Abuela, grilling savory meats and watching her brothers fight over the last cold brew. Anything beat listening to her father's latest idea about how he could save the restaurant money by washing and reusing their straws.

In her previous life as a teacher, Mari had dealt with bothersome parents, impossible co-workers, and student fights. And now, the only fights she ever broke up were between her dad and Mr. Chun, the owner of the Chinese restaurant across the street. They had a rivalry that dated back to Mari's childhood.

These were the reasons that Mari needed some space. She needed somewhere besides her dumpy one-bedroom apartment that was ten minutes away from the restaurant to relax after a hard day's work. Besides that, she'd been saving for a place that was much nicer. Maybe even a place with a community pool.

Mari hadn't told her parents she was thinking about moving. But secretly she had been apartment hunting with her friend Jemina. Jemina was all in favor of Mari moving somewhere new. Somewhere nicer. Somewhere farther away from the restaurant and her parent's house.

A week later Mari announced that she was moving into a newer and fancier apartment on the west side of town. At around the same time, her friend Jemina had suggested inviting a few friends over for a housewarming party. Jemina had also convinced Mari not to invite her family this time, specifically her brothers Alex and David. Last time her brothers had attended a house party, they'd shown up late, had eaten an entire pizza, and then they'd left without so much as a thank you.

"I will handle your brothers if they show up uninvited," Jemina said on the night of Mari's housewarming party. "This is going to be fun. I've invited a few friends from work, and you still haven't met Bianca, my new roommate. It's about time you made some friends of your own."

"So you keep telling me," Mari replied. She didn't have many friends outside of work apart from Jemina and Officer Rick Kinney, the police officer she'd been dating off and on for the last year.

Rick and Jemina had come over early to help Mari with the food. Stirred into a frenzy by the scent of the fruit tarts, cinnamon bundt cake, and pecan pie that Mari had spent the morning making, her bulldog Tabasco ran back and forth yipping excitedly.

"Calm down, Tabasco, or you're going to stir up trouble," Mari said as she came into the kitchen carrying a stack of pizza boxes and several bags of groceries. "I bought chips, nuts, and some other finger foods. Do you think that's enough?"

"It's plenty," Rick responded, holding out a maple-bacon-flavored dog treat for Tabasco. "We're not expecting a hundred people."

"Is queso dip like a Texan thing?" Jemina asked, who was loading drinks into an ice chest. "I tried explaining it to my friend Aimée Carver from Connecticut, and she didn't know what I was talking about.'"

"I'm pretty sure she knows what queso dip is," Rick said. "Some people just like playing dumb. Aimée included."

"You know Aimée Carver?" Jemina asked.

Rick nodded. "She works at that boutique, right? Mai Hair Salon or something like that?"

"Chi Hair Salon," she corrected him.

"Right." Rick shrugged. "I had to interview her and Bianca last summer after a string of robberies down that way."

Mari hadn't been expecting a hundred people, or even fifty, but when half an hour had passed, she began to worry that no one was going to show up. She was relieved when Bianca arrived, wearing an emerald green dress studded with rhinestones. Bianca was followed a few minutes later by Aimée Carver and her boyfriend Carlos, a beefy, broad-shouldered man with dark beady eyes.

"I thought you said this was a nice apartment," Aimée commented in a suspiciously stereotypical French accent.

Rick scoffed in surprise and nearly choked on a chip.

But Mari, with unwavering calm, winked at him and said, "You should have seen the one I had before."

Everyone present laughed except Aimée, who continued to glare at Mari's modest furniture.

"This might be nice for Texas," Aimée said, "but where I come from we call it *low-income housing*." Pointing a shaky finger at Tabasco, who was leaping around playfully at her feet, she asked, "What is that thing?"

"Us humble Texas folk call that a *dog*," Rick cleverly replied.

Aimée pretended not to hear him. She'd been bothered since the moment her name was spoken. "I told you, it's *Aimée*. Not Amy. It's pronounced the French way, okay."

An uncomfortable silence followed during which Mari noticed Carlos standing behind Aimée. He tugged at the collar of his polo and eyed Bianca's emerald dress.

"If I had known this was a costume party, I would have brought my Iron Man suit," Carlos said.

Bianca laughed and blushed modestly. "What can I say? I wear what I want, and this dress needed a night out. Of course, my style is nothing compared to Aimée's."

Aimée, who was standing at the table helping herself to chips and dip, sniffed haughtily. She didn't seem to care that Mari hadn't invited her guests to help themselves yet. Aimée frowned as a bit of queso dip dripped down her blouse.

"Where I come from, you have to dress nice," Aimée said. "People take you seriously when you dress nice."

"And does it work for you?" asked Rick slyly.

Aimée paused with a chip halfway to her mouth. "Does what work for me?"

"Do people actually take you seriously?" Rick boldly asked.

Aimée's cheeks turned crimson, and it looked like she was about to rain fury on Rick when Mari intervened. "How are the chips, Aimée?" she asked, taking care to say her name the French way.

"They are not horrible," she replied with characteristic tact. "But this cheese dip is fantastic. I must admit I have a weakness for cheese."

"Everyone knows that," Bianca commented quietly.

"Lucky for me I have this all to myself right now," Aimée said, clutching the queso bowl protectively. It didn't seem to have occurred to her that everyone had brought food to the buffet except her. Surveying the bottled drinks on the table, Aimée let out a noise of disgust. "Do you have anything better?"

"Bottled water," Jemina responded.

Mari glanced from Aimée to Carlos and shook her head in disbelief. He seemed like a decent enough person, and she couldn't fathom how the two of them had ended up together.

Tabasco continued to tag along behind Aimée everywhere she went. Feeling sure she had heard a knock, Mari walked over to the front of the room and opened the door.

"Wanda," she said. "Please, come in."

Wanda Hill was an older woman who lived in the apartment next door. Mari had introduced herself a couple of days ago. Wanda's place was filled with the stench and squawks of parakeets, and Wanda's cross-stitching projects covered most of the walls.

"I don't want to come in, thanks," Wanda said, thrusting her graying head inside. "I just heard a lot of noise that made it hard to hear the television. At my age it puts a strain on my eyes, trying to read subtitles. I would turn the volume up, but then Agnes who lives to my left would come over and complain."

"I'm sure that would be awful," Mari replied with understated sarcasm. "I'm sorry about the noise. We'll try to keep it down."

"Thank you," Wanda said. She turned to leave but paused in the hallway. "Oh, and one more thing. What time is this party over?"

"No later than ten," Mari answered.

"Good, because you remember the rule—"

"I remember," Mari cut in. "There is ten o'clock noise curfew. No noisiness after ten. You won't have to worry, I promise."

Wanda forced a smile and returned to her apartment. Mari shut the door with a deep sense of relief and returned to her guests. Carlos was standing at the snack table chatting with a slender young man with a thick head of wavy black hair. He was Austin Murphy, another on of Jemina's co-workers. Austin was nattily dressed in a sports coat and a pair of khakis. Carlos's girlfriend Aimée, however, was nowhere to be seen.

"Where's Aimée?" Mari asked him.

"Still in the kitchen, I think," Carlos responded, not looking overly concerned. "I heard her a minute ago yelling at the dog."

"That's *all* I need," Mari muttered under her breath. But at that moment the air was rent by a scream and Jemina came running from the kitchen looking sickly pale.

Mari ran in, fearing the worst. Aimée lay flat on her back on the floor in front of the refrigerator.

"Aimée?" Mari said. But Aimée neither spoke nor moved.

Carlos and Austin came running in together a second later.

"What happened?" Carlos asked, kneeling down at Aimée's side. "Did she pass out?"

"No, she hasn't fainted," Jemina said. "Mari, I'm so sorry. I thought a party was a good idea. I really did."

"I don't believe it," said Carlos in a dazed voice. "She's not breathing at all."

"Of course she's not," Jemina blurted out. "She's dead."

## CHAPTER TWO

Carlos rose slowly from the floor and staggered over to the sink. He turned on the faucet and began clutching his stomach while the rest of the guests glanced at each other with wide, fearful eyes. No one had particularly liked Aimée, but seeing her on the kitchen floor was quite a shock for everyone.

"I'll call the detective," Rick said. "No one touch anything." Rick pulled out his cell phone and called the station. He seemed to be the only one with a level head at the moment.

"Well, after this," Jemina muttered, "I wouldn't blame you if you moved." She was standing at Mari's elbow clutching a plastic cup filled with grape soda. "Death seems to stalk you, doesn't it?"

"It's never followed me home before," Mari replied, watching Bianca lead Carlos into the living room. He looked pale and sweaty, and his hands were trembling nervously. "Maybe it was an accident?"

"I hope so," Jemina agreed.

Mari sighed. "I can't believe this."

This was exactly what Mari had hoped to avoid by moving. She shook her head and came to the conclusion that she was cursed. She didn't know how but for some reason trouble would not leave her alone. Even when she moved.

"We have to find out what happened," Jemina whispered. Taking Mari by the hand, she began tugging her in the direction of the living room. "You talk to Carlos while I question Austin."

"Austin?" Mari asked. "Oh, right. Sorry, I only met him briefly when the party started." Mari took a deep breath. "Are you sure that's a good idea?"

"Of course I'm sure." Jemina frowned. "You of all people should want to know what happened in your own house."

"Fine," Mari agreed. "But only because I need the peace of mind of knowing that this really was an accident. Are you sure Aimée didn't have heart problems or something like that?"

"Not as far as I know." Jemina shook her head. She gestured toward Austin Murphy. "Austin works with me at Woofle's Snack Company. Marketing division. Always overdressed and, if you ask me, a little too flirty. It is probably best if I talk to him."

"Wave at me if he starts coming onto you," Mari said.

"I can handle him," Jemina said with a wink, and she walked away.

Mari found Carlos sitting on the couch slowly stroking his face with his hands. His eyes were glossy, but he wasn't crying. Bianca placed one hand on his shoulder and whispered words of comfort. He was paying her little attention.

Mari sat down on the other side of Carlos. "I'm really sorry about Aimée," she said. How did one even begin a conversation with a man moments after his girlfriend died? "You must be devastated."

"Shocked, mostly," Carlos replied. "We had only been going out for a few weeks." He turned and looked at her suspiciously. "You seem awfully calm about the whole thing."

Mari shrugged. "I didn't know her as well as you did. We had only just met through Jemina." She neglected to mention that she had also seen her fair share of bodies. "Have you ever lost anyone close?"

Carlos shook his head. "Only my grandma. But that was a long time ago, and I was too young to understand really. I remember standing there as her casket was lowered into the ground. It was rainy, and all I could think about was how I wanted it to end so I could eat one of the sandwiches on the reception table."

"I think we're all fairly sheltered from the reality of death when we're young," Mari said. Carlos nodded solemnly.

At that moment Tabasco barked, and Rick came striding into the living room waving a cell phone in one hand. "Detective Price is downstairs wandering around in the parking lot. Hold down the fort, will you, until I get back?"

"Sure," Mari responded. "Hey, where's the ambulance?"

"On its way," Rick answered. "We'll be down there waiting for them."

But as soon as Rick had opened the door, a couple of paramedics in blue uniforms swarmed into the living room. They dragged a stretcher behind them. A second later, Detective Price swept into the apartment briskly in his usual suit and tie.

"Any luck?" Detective Price asked as he came into the kitchen, where one of the paramedics was bent over her.

"No luck reviving her," the paramedic said. "She's completely gone."

Detective Price hung his head. "Obviously she's going to need a coroner's examination, but what's your first impression?"

"Just looking at her, I couldn't tell you," the paramedic replied, wiping his sweaty brow with the back of one arm. "There's no evidence of physical injury or blunt trauma."

"Could she have died of natural causes?" the detective asked.

"At her age? That's not likely, Detective." The paramedic covered Aimée's face out of respect. "The coroner will give you the answers, Sir."

While Detective Price and Rick stood talking in the seclusion of the kitchen,

Jemina came striding over. "It's just so sad," she said. "I think up until the moment the paramedics pronounced her dead, Carlos still had some hope. Now he just looks crushed."

Jemina motioned to the couch, where Carlos was still sitting in what appeared to be a lethargic state.

"I think he'll be fine," Mari replied. "Or he will be, in an hour or two. What did you see when you went into the kitchen, Jemina?"

"I didn't see much." Jemina scratched her head, trying to recall the details. "One-second Aimée was standing at the sink opening one of the water bottles—it was sealed pretty tightly, so she was using a knife to loosen the cap—and the next second she just fell over. At first, I thought maybe she had fainted or had cut herself with the knife. But there was no blood, and then she wasn't breathing…"

"Bizarre," Mari mumbled.

Jemina nodded. "It was like that day my boss died." Jemina's boss had dropped dead at an office party a few months earlier after ingesting poison. "I didn't even particularly like the guy, but that was still a terrible thing to witness. And when I saw Aimée laying there all those memories came flooding back. Honestly, I don't know how you can go through this again and again without being traumatized. You must have a heart of steel."

"Or of stone," Mari joked. Jemina scoffed.

The relative tranquility and enjoyment of the party had been radically disrupted by Aimée's death. Now the guests wandered listlessly around the room or sat motionless as if contemplating their own mortality. The only person who seemed to have been unaffected by it was Austin, Jemina's co-worker, who stood at the table piling a small Styrofoam plate full of mixed nuts, nachos, and queso dip. He looked about as excited as Carlos must have been after his grandmother's funeral. Mari saw Bianca staring at him from a few feet away, her brows knitted in distaste, muttering under her breath.

Detective Price, who had been watching him out of the corner of his eye, raised his voice in alarm. "NO!" the detective shouted.

Austin dropped the plate and raised his hands in surprise.

"Sorry," Austin blurted out. "I was hungry and well ... this is a party."

"This apartment is a crime scene, and everything must be carefully examined, including the food. You must touch none of it." Detective Price nudged him out of the way. Tabasco trotted at his heels. "And someone put that dog in his kennel. I won't have him messing with my crime scene too."

Mari reluctantly did as the detective directed and shut Tabasco in her room. She returned to her guests after a moment of silence to collect her thoughts.

"Do you think," Jemina said to Mari in a low voice, "that Aimée might have been poisoned?"

Mari shook her head. "No way. I made all the food myself, and none of it has been out of my sight."

"You made an awful lot of queso dip," Jemina commented.

"*One* bowl," Mari replied.

"One?" Jemina raised her eyebrows. "I saw two when I went into the kitchen. I suspect some of your guests brought food as well."

That certainly could have been true. Mari threw a swift glance at the table where the snacks were sitting. Austin had only just opened the package of nuts, and most of the other dips hadn't even been touched. The one exception was the queso dip, which Aimée had been eating before she died.

"I didn't make that queso that Aimée was eating," Mari said.

"Do you think that dip was meant for Aimée or someone else at the party?" Jemina asked.

"I have no idea," Mari answered. "Let's find out who brought it."

## CHAPTER THREE

Carlos was still sitting on the couch, twiddling his thumbs as he waited for the detective's permission to leave. Every now and again his eyes would fall on the glass of water Bianca had poured him in an effort to calm his nerves. He picked the glass up nervously before setting it down again.

"It's okay, you can drink it," Bianca told him. "I poured it from a sealed bottle."

"Still," he replied, "I think it's best not to take any chances."

Mari sat down next to him. As always, her desire to be a comforting presence fought with her need to find out who had committed the murder. "You said you had only been going out for a couple of weeks," she stated. "How long had y'all known each other?"

"Not much longer than that," Carlos replied in a monotonous voice. He didn't seem bothered by the repeated questions, but he also didn't seem particularly invested in the conversation. Picking up the glass and holding it in his hands without drinking, he added, "I work at one of the local delis, Ham & Please, and late last summer Aimée started coming in during her lunch hour. She and Austin were always together, and I remember the first time I saw her, thinking how pretty she was and how it was all wasted on a guy like that. I really thought they were dating. It wasn't until later that she mentioned being single."

"And one thing led to another," Mari guessed.

"Yeah," Carlos quietly responded. "We started going out a couple of days later."

"And you had a good relationship?"

To her surprise, Carlos shrugged. "I mean, I guess. She was pretty, easy to talk to, and she had the most interesting stories about her worldly travels."

He stopped, having presumably exhausted the list of Aimée's good qualities. Mari had the feeling that he was holding something back. Carlos seemed oddly reserved and withdrawn, and she wondered if it was because he was having trouble absorbing the shock of her death.

"Well," she said, beginning to rise from the couch, "I'm sorry your relationship had to end this way. You shouldn't have to bury someone you've only known for a couple of months. That's—"

"Mari?" Carlos interrupted. "It's sweet of you to offer your condolences, but I'm okay. I'll be fine in a day or two."

"Sorry," Mari said, feeling tremendously awkward. "I just thought—"

He rose from the couch, stretched, and finally took a sip of water. "I'm just feeling a little antsy because I have to get to bed early. I've got an early shift tomorrow, and I'm tired."

"Right." Mari couldn't believe how quickly he'd changed his tune. An hour prior, he'd been white with shock. "By the way, Carlos, thank you for bringing … I'm sorry, what was it that you brought tonight?"

"Cold cuts," Carlos replied as if the answer were obvious. "Nothing but the deli's bestsellers."

As Carlos chatted with a policeman about leaving the crime scene, Jemina joined Mari. She cleared her throat and glanced around the apartment.

"I wonder what that relationship was *really* like," Mari said to Jemina, who was struggling to open another water bottle. "Do you think they were even that serious?"

"Too early to tell, don't you think? Ugh. Why are these things so hard to open?" Jemina stamped her foot in frustration, drawing the stares of Rick and Detective Price.

"Here," Mari said, reaching for the bottle and opening it with ease. Jemina raised her eyebrows. "I fought off two brothers every day as a kid. Any luck with Austin?"

Jemina shook her head in disgust. "None so far. He just complimented my outfit and asked if I wanted to hit up the pool hall after the police let us leave. Apparently, it's ladies' night, and there's a live band playing."

"So you're going?"

"Of course not," Jemina said, looking aghast. Mari chuckled. "I'm going to do some more digging before the detective calls it a night. I suggest that you do the same."

Mari found Bianca in the living room singing an old lullaby to one of Mari's aloe plants. "You know they say if you sing to them," Bianca said, "it actually helps them grow faster. My parents have their own greenhouse back in Louisiana, but they're getting old and they've been talking about passing it down to me."

"How long did you know Aimée?" Mari asked.

"Since she started working at Chi's. It must have been about a year ago now. Has it been that long? I took her under my wing and trained her. She can seem harsh when you first meet her, but once you get to know her, she's just as sweet as can be. Once when I was in the hospital she brought me a pecan pie, and a six-pack of those fruity, fizzy drinks because she knew I loved those."

"Did your customers like her?" Mari continued.

"Well enough, I guess," Bianca responded, scratching the back of her neck. "We had a couple of minor incidents the first week because she insisted on doing everyone's hair the French way, and some of our girls don't like having their hair done that way. At one point she threatened to walk out, but I talked her into staying. Where else was she going to find work around here?"

"And everything went smoothly after that?" Mari waited patiently for an explanation.

Bianca frowned as if weighing the question in her mind. "To tell you the truth, she had been acting odd the last couple of weeks. Not like herself at all."

"Odd? How?" Mari asked.

"More than once she came into work with her hair frazzled and uncombed, looking like it hadn't been washed. Her shirt wasn't tucked in and her clothes looked like they had been slept in. I took her aside and talked to her about it. Told her that we expected more out of her, and that I wanted her to look her best for work."

"How did she respond?" Mari watched as Bianca paused and took a deep breath.

"You know Aimée," Bianca said. "Well, you *did*. She could never admit to making a mistake. She said she would consider my suggestion, but after that she came in well-dressed. We never talked about it again."

"Thanks, Bianca. Hey, by the way, what appetizer did you bring tonight? I want to make sure everyone gets their dishes back."

"The sugar cookies," Bianca said with a guilty expression. "I didn't have time to make them myself, so I ran by the store on my way here. I hope that was okay."

"Fine," Mari replied. "Thanks for coming, Bianca. Sorry about all this."

As she was walking back toward the kitchen to reconvene with Jemina, Mari felt a tap on her arm. It was Austin, and he was eyeing her in that odd flirtatious way that Jemina had warned her about.

"Hey, listen," Austin said. "It's a shame about what happened to your party. I'm sorry it ended so abruptly."

"That's okay," Mari said in a level tone. "I'm more worried about the circumstances under which it ended."

This didn't seem to have occurred to Austin, and he stood staring at her for a moment in confusion.

"I'm guessing you didn't know Aimée very well?" Mari asked.

Austin shook his head. "Nope, we had just met. Hey, just to make it up to you, what do you say we go and get drinks after wor ... I mean, after this place clears out."

Mari narrowed her eyes.

"Thanks," she said. "I'm good. By the way, what appetizer did you bring to the party? Silly little me just forgot."

"Queso dip," Austin replied. "It goes great with tortilla chips. You should give it a try."

## CHAPTER FOUR

Standing on the threshold of the kitchen, Mari paused and surveyed her apartment. Aimée's body had already been carried out in a body bag. Carlos had left. Bianca and Austin were standing together talking by the aloe plant in the living room while Tabasco knelt beside them gnawing on a slice of beef jerky. Detective Price was talking quietly on his phone while Jemina busied herself rinsing plates in the kitchen.

"Any thoughts?" Mari asked, grabbing a hand towel and beginning to dry dishes.

Jemina shook her head. "Not really. Bianca seems to have known Aimée best, and it's hard to imagine Bianca ever lifting a finger in anger."

"Austin brought the queso dip, but I'm hesitant to point any fingers," Mari responded. "He still seems to be looking for someone to sleep with, even in light of what just happened. He doesn't strike me as the murderer type. Just lousy husband material."

"They never do, at first," Jemina commented.

Detective Price came over and clapped a rough hand on Mari's shoulder. "We are finished here," he said. "I'll come by the restaurant tomorrow around opening. Make me one of those big enchilada platters, the kind that can feed a family of five. Have it waiting for me when I get there."

"Will do," Mari agreed.

The detective stopped at the table in the living room to talk to Rick on his way out. Rick was busily bagging all the open containers so that he could take them back to the station to be tested. While Mari stood at the kitchen counter straining to hear what they were saying, the front door opened unexpectedly. Tabasco rose up on all fours, his teeth bared, growling quietly.

"Tabasco, calm down," Mari shouted as she ran into the living room. She was relieved to see that it was just Wanda, curlers in her hair.

"Please keep it down in here," Wanda demanded in an irritated voice. "My favorite show is on, and my parakeets won't stop squawking. They get excited when there are things going on next door." Seeing Detective Price, she added, "Hello, Officer."

"Ma'am," Detective Price replied, taking her gently by the shoulders, "there's been a death this evening. I would appreciate your full cooperation." Wanda let out a low gasp, and her face whitened. "I knew you would understand."

Wanda looked stunned. She seemed to have thought the police were just making a friendly visit. When her shock subsided, Mari saw her face shift from confusion to suspicion.

"Nothing like this has ever happened in this building before," she said quietly. She looked into Mari's face, her eyes narrowed. "Never, in the twenty years I've lived here. Then you move in and all of a sudden someone dies."

"Alright, that's enough," Detective Price said. "I can assure you that Mari will be nothing but a pleasant neighbor." He cleared his throat and glanced at Tabasco. "That dog, however ..."

Wanda sniffed. "Well, you're not off to a good start, as far as I can tell."

All this while Tabasco had gone on growling as though sensing the fear and disdain radiating off of Wanda. Mari threw him a warning glare.

"Listen," Mari said, but stopped when she looked up and saw the expression on Wanda's face. She didn't look afraid or angry. On the contrary, she watched Rick and Detective Price with an expression of deep absorption. It was the same sort of expression Mari had seen on the faces of friends when they were watching an especially interesting TV show.

It occurred to Mari that Wanda probably wasn't used to seeing real-life drama. This must have been more exciting for her than an episode of her favorite soap opera.

"Wanda, why don't you come in and sit down?" she asked. "There's plenty of room."

Wanda nodded gratefully and moved into the living room, glancing cautiously around as if afraid she might accidentally sit down on a piece of evidence. Tabasco didn't let her out of his sight.

"Nice place," Wanda commented. "I mean, for a crime scene."

"Wanda, why don't you come over for dinner tomorrow night?" Mari suggested, hoping that Wanda would benefit from a friendly dose of hospitality.

Wanda hesitated as if torn between the longing for a free meal and the desire to stay in her own apartment where no deaths had taken place. "Are you sure it will be safe?"

Mari nodded. "Of course. Don't be silly. It'll just be me and Tabasco." She glanced down at her eager bulldog. "Well, maybe just me."

"I think I would like that, actually," Wanda replied. "It's been a long time since anyone has invited me to dinner." She took a deep breath and glanced in the kitchen. "Besides, you can tell me all about the party. I'll figure out whodunit in a heartbeat. I've seen lots of detective shows."

"Isn't that nice," the detective muttered.

"You eat meat, right?" Mari continued, ignoring the detective. "I'll slow-cook a pork roast, and maybe some sides from the restaurant to go with it."

Wanda nodded eagerly, and the excitement was now plain on her face. She stood up to leave as if her purpose for visiting had been served. "See you tomorrow."

Mari rubbed her forehead as Wanda left.

"That went well," Jemina said in a low voice as she entered the living room. "Good luck with that one. Neighbors can be tricky. This is why I usually avoid speaking to mine."

"I hope this works," Mari responded. "I also hope she doesn't expect me to cook her dinner every time things get too rowdy."

"Never let your brothers come over, and you'll be fine." Jemina chuckled. "What compelled you to offer *dinner* of things anyway?"

"Because I can't be having trouble with the neighbors already, not three days after I move in," Mari stated. "I don't want Wanda gossiping to the other neighbors about me. A small gesture of kindness will go a long way toward keeping her mouth shut."

"I didn't know you were such a strategic thinker," Jemina said, sounding impressed.

"I didn't use to be," Mari added quietly.

"I'll drink to that," Jemina replied, returning to the kitchen for a cold brew.

## CHAPTER FIVE

Mari stayed up much of the night and only managed a couple hours of sleep before she had to get up for work. She stumbled through the morning shift at her family's restaurant feeling scattered and foggy like she was wandering numbly through a dream. A gray fog had settled over the streets and alleys of town, contributing to her eerie mood.

After everyone had left last night, minus her friend Jemina, Mari had made tea and sat at the table for about an hour discussing the case. It had been Jemina who had first raised the suggestion that maybe the murderer had killed Aimée by mistake. That had left Mari with even more questions. If Aimée hadn't been the intended victim, then who was? Had Mari been the intended target? Or maybe Jemina or even Rick?

Mari and Jemina had argued back and forth for some time as to who the killer had meant to kill. She hadn't been sure when she'd gone to bed. And here in the cold light of morning, Mari felt as perplexed as ever. The only thing she knew for certain was that Aimée was dead. She wouldn't know for sure that the queso dip had been poisoned until the results came back from the station. In the meantime, she and the rest of her guests were in limbo, wondering what had happened and why.

David and Alex, Mari's younger adult brothers, came into the restaurant while Mari mindlessly filled salt shakers.

"You're not looking too well," Alex commented. "Up late last night?"

"We all know how much you like to party," David added in a sarcastic tone. The last time she and her brothers had gone to a party, Mari had complained the whole way there about wanting to be in bed with a book.

"You wouldn't happen to have any leftovers, would you?" Alex asked. "I know how much food you made, and there's no way your guests ate all of that."

"I'm sure it all would have been consumed if you two had been there," Mari said. "In which case, both of you would probably be dead."

Alex and David looked at each, and then quickly sat down. Mari told them about Aimée's death and Detective Price's suggestion that the food might have been poisoned.

"Lesson learned I guess," David commented. "Never eat the food at a party where Mari is the host."

Mari rolled her eyes. "Anyway, neither one of you are starving. I seem to recall you both owning your own food truck, not to mention the fact that you both practically live in the kitchen. Dad is keeping a tally of all the free meals you cook yourselves."

"Yeah, but your food is different," Alex said. "*You* try telling Dad that you're sick of eating Mexican food all day. I know you made biscuits."

"I didn't make biscuits." Mari shook her head.

"Whatever," Alex continued. "We got our fix somewhere else."

"Surely you didn't—"

"Dad will never know." Alex tilted his head toward the window. Across the street sat the Lucky Noodle. It had good Chinese food, but it was also owned by José Ramirez's number one rival, Mr. Chun.

"And you won't tell him," David added. "Now, there's a good sister."

"Yes, you would be wise to keep it from dad," Alex went on. "I only *just* recovered the hearing in my left ear. You don't want me to go deaf, do you?"

"Call us next time you make pie," David suggested.

Mari rolled her eyes again.

At that moment, Mr. Ramirez came walking out of his office at the back of the restaurant muttering under his breath. When he saw Tabasco lying on his paws under the table, he gave him a serious look.

"Mari, you live in a very nice apartment now. I see no reason why you should bring that animal to work anymore." Mr. Ramirez crossed his arms.

Mari's face turned rosy but before she could object Mr. Ramirez held up a hand to quiet her.

"But—"

"That wasn't what I came out here to talk to you about," he interrupted, looking earnestly from Mari's face to those of his two sons. There was a zeal in his eyes that had never portended well in the past.

"What's going on, Dad?" Mari asked with an uneasy feeling.

"Nothing to worry about, I can assure you," Mr. Ramirez replied, ignoring their skeptical glances. "You're going to love what I'm about to propose. Not only because it's cool and techy, which I hear the kids love these days, but because it's about to save us a ton of money. And I know how much you love saving money."

"I really do, Dad," Alex muttered sarcastically.

"I have decided," Mr. Ramirez went on, raising his hands high, "to install motion sensor lights in the kitchen and the bathrooms."

He paused, as though waiting for Mari, David, and Alex to erupt in applause. Instead, Alex struggled to suppress a snicker while Mari pretended to entertain the idea thoughtfully.

"That sounds great, Dad," she said. "I mean … why? Why are we doing this?"

"To save money," Mr. Ramirez stated. "I thought I made that clear from the beginning. There is no bigger drain on our income than the amount of money we spend paying for electricity we don't even use. I can't count the number of times I've come in here before work to find that the kitchen light, the office light, or the hall light had been left on by whoever closed the night before." He held up one hand as though expecting another outcry. "I'm not trying to spread blame. If we get motion sensor lights, the lights will *only* come on when there is actually someone in the room."

"I understand how motion sensor lights work," Mari added. "And I think that's a great idea for the office, but the kitchen? I don't know. That seems like it could be dangerous."

Mr. Ramirez grunted, suggesting that he didn't care. Just then the front door opened and Mrs. Ramirez came in, followed, a second later, by Detective Price.

"Do you have a few minutes?" the detective said to Mari. "This won't take long."

Mr. Ramirez glanced uneasily back and forth from Mari to the detective. "Is something wrong, detective?" he asked.

"Nothing y'all aren't already familiar with," Detective Price replied. "Just a few questions about a murder at Mari's housewarming party last night."

## CHAPTER SIX

Silence fell over the room for a moment, and Mr. Ramirez looked stiff. Of course, Mari had planned on telling him about the incident at her new apartment sooner, but he had been so absorbed in his new idea that there hadn't been time to bring it up. Fully expecting his wrath to rain down on her, she shut her eyes and waited for the shouting.

"Housewarming party?" he repeated. "You threw a housewarming party, and you didn't invite your own family?"

"It was Jemina's idea," Mari replied. "It was just going to be a small party, and I didn't want all the food to disappear before the other guests arrived. No offense."

"Unacceptable," Mr. Ramirez said. His eyes twinkled, and Mari had a funny suspicion that he was teasing her. "But since none of us were there, that means *we're* not under investigation for once. Is that right, Detective?"

"Currently none of you are under suspicion," Detective Price answered. "But Mari, I do need to know exactly what foods you prepared last night."

Mari had to think about it. The shock of the murder had driven the preparations for the party straight out of her mind. "I made some appetizers, a pecan pie, a cinnamon bundt cake, and some fancy looking fruit tarts. There were some other things I picked up from the store on my way home too. I'll have to look at my receipts."

"Was Aimée a close friend of yours?"

Mari shook her head. "Not at all. I know it's hard to believe in a town this small, but I hadn't met her until last night."

"So she would have had no reason to kill her," Mr. Ramirez interjected. "You don't have to be a detective to come to that conclusion."

"Thank you, Mr. Ramirez," Detective Price responded. "When did you first notice there was something wrong with Ms. Carver?"

"She looked perfectly fine up until the moment she collapsed. She went into the kitchen to get some bottled water because the sodas I had set out in the living room didn't appeal to her. Then Jemina screamed, and the next thing I knew, Aimée was sprawled out on the floor of my kitchen. By the time I got to her, she wasn't breathing."

"And the queso dip," he continued. "You're one hundred percent sure it wasn't yours?"

"The one she ate from wasn't mine," Mari replied. "I'm certain of that."

"Do you have any idea who brought it?"

"Austin Murphy." Mari nodded matter-of-factly. "He told me so himself. I also just met him last night. He and Jemina work together." She gave the detective a suspicious look. "So, it really was the queso that killed her?"

Detective Price set down his notepad and folded his arms. "Preliminary results suggest that the queso may have been laced with cyanide. We may be looking at a premeditated homicide."

Mari gasped, and her two brothers exchanged worried glances.

"There's something else I've been wondering about." Mari gulped, her heart racing. "Do you think the murderer intended to kill Aimée? Is it possible that the poison was meant for someone else?"

"To be quite honest with you, Mari," Detective Price answered, "It is possible. The moment I learn anything, I'll let you know." He cleared his throat. "And Mari ..."

"Yes, detective," Mari responded.

"I'm only sharing this information with you because I know you'll go snooping either way." The detective shook his head.

"For once though, just stay out of this one. Okay?"

***

"But if Austin brought the queso, and the queso was poisoned," Mari said to Jemina, "that means you could be working with a killer. He might even have been trying to kill *you*."

Mari and Jemina were hunched over together in a corner booth at the restaurant. It was Jemina's lunch hour, and she'd ordered spicy shrimp enchiladas. Mari had decided to join her.

"That's entirely possible," Jemina replied in between bites, not looking pleased at the prospect. "Though to be honest, I think Austin would rather make out with me than kill me."

"But the queso was his," Mari reiterated. "He brought the queso to the party, and the queso was poisoned, so—"

"I wish it were that simple," Jemina cut in, reaching for a napkin, "but the fact is that we don't know when the queso was poisoned. It was left out on the table for some time after Austin's arrival."

Mari sucked on her straw thoughtfully. It hadn't occurred to her that the queso might have been poisoned during the party because she had assumed there would be too many eyes on the table. "There were at least six people in that living room at all times," she stated. "If the queso was tampered with, someone was bound to have seen it."

"Maybe someone did see it," Jemina added.

Mari studied her quizzically. "You mean Aimée? If she had seen someone poisoning the queso, why would she have eaten it?"

"No, not Aimée," Jemina clarified. "But maybe someone else did. Maybe they are staying quiet because they're afraid the murderer will come after them if they speak up."

This was certainly possible, but it brought them no closer to solving the mystery. In fact, it left them with another one. In addition to looking for the murderer, they were now searching for anyone who might have seen the murderer at work.

"The police investigation is moving way too slowly," Mari went on.

"Be patient, Mari. I know it's tough when the crime went down in your own apartment, but you have to let the police do their job."

"I know, but it's hard to just sit here," Mari responded. "I think it might be time we started doing some digging of our own. Anyone who knew Aimée might be able to shed some light on her past. I would love to know how a woman like her ended up in a small town in Texas for one."

"Then I know where we need to start looking," Jemina commented. "We should start with the one person out of all the guests who knew her best."

"Carlos?" Mari asked.

Jemina shook her head. "No, not Carlos. Bianca. I'm heading over to Chi at five, and you're welcome to come along. I have a few questions I would like to ask her. I have a sneaking suspicion that Bianca and Aimée weren't as close as I thought they were."

## CHAPTER SEVEN

After lunch, Jemina returned to work and the rest of the afternoon dragged by slowly. Mari was eager to begin her investigation, which made it all the more frustrating that she had been assigned to wash dishes in the kitchen. More than once her father walked past to inspect the plates she had just finished drying; mentioning that they could be cleaner.

"This isn't your way of punishing me for not loving your motion sensor idea, is it?" she asked him.

Mr. Ramirez shook his head. "Although now that you mention it—" He handed her a glass with an unsightly water stain. Mari swore under her breath and continued scrubbing.

Mari finally left the restaurant at a quarter to five. It was a remarkably warm day, and the air smelled strongly of fresh cut grass. It was the time of year she associated with being young and in love—her ex-boyfriend had proposed to her on an afternoon just like this one. As she drove toward Chi Hair Salon, she saw a couple walking down the street holding hands and pushing a stroller while shop owners swept their outdoor patios in preparation for the evening rush.

Jemina was waiting for her outside the salon when she arrived ten minutes later. From the outside it was a nondescript building in a rundown strip mall, so Mari was surprised to find the interior decorated fancy with white walls, white floors, framed mirrors, a large cut-glass chandelier, and potted plants tall enough for a grown man to hide behind. The smell of perfume was overpowering, and it took Mari a full minute to adjust to it.

Bianca stood at the far edge of the room where a small boutique had been set up. She wore a semi-transparent dress that looked like it was made out of bubble wrap with a vibrant pink dress underneath. A pair of red high-heeled shoes matched her handbag, and she wore four shining several rings, two on each hand, that reflected the overhead lights. Mari had to hand it to Bianca. She didn't think Bianca could top last night's outfit, but she had.

"I thought you might be coming by," Bianca said, clicking her rings together so that they made a harsh, grating sound that set Mari's teeth on edge. "That nosy detective was just in here, and he warned me not to talk to you. Would you like to look at our new boutique section?"

Mari shook her head. "I just need to ask you a few questions, and then I'll be out of your hair. Do you know anyone, or can you think of anyone, who might have had a grudge against Aimée?"

"And why should I help you when the detective told me not to?" Bianca asked.

"Oh, my," Jemina said as she began walking through Bianca's display of blouses. "What a beautiful store. I might even make a purchase."

"Yes," Mari chimed in awkwardly. "What she said."

"Fine. I'll help you." Bianca frowned pensively. "Aimée got along fine with the other employees. As far as her personal life, I couldn't tell you. She kept to herself and never spoke much about her home life." She grated her rings together again before taking a deep breath.

Mari nodded. "Did she have any close friends that you know of?"

"Oh, lots of acquaintances," Bianca replied. "And lots of enemies. That woman was a drama magnet. But I can't think of a single person who would have hated her enough to want to kill her. She wouldn't like me saying this, but she was actually quite an ordinary person."

"Bianca," Jemina chimed in, "you mentioned last night that Aimée hadn't been acting like herself for the past couple of weeks coming in late and lazily dressed. Do you have any idea what might have been going on?"

Bianca shook her head sadly. "I couldn't tell you. Maybe her boyfriend knows."

"Do you think they were fighting?" Jemina asked. "Did she ever mention anything about Carlos?"

"Once, I think," Bianca replied. "But she didn't go on about him the way some of the girls do about their boyfriends. In fact, it was almost like she purposefully avoided the subject completely at times."

"Really," Mari muttered, the wheels in her head turning.

"If my memory serves me right," Bianca replied. "I asked her once if she was okay."

"How did she respond?" Mari looked to Jemina eagerly.

"Not good, of course. That was a while ago when I decided to just stay out of her way." Bianca shrugged. "As long as she showed up for work we didn't speak a whole lot."

Glancing up at the clock, Mari was alarmed to find that it was almost six o'clock. "Darn. I have to run. I have dinner plans."

"Ah yes," Jemina muttered. "Wanda, the curious neighbor."

Mari thanked Bianca and turned toward the exit. "I have to stop by the restaurant to pick up food, and I'm already going to be late getting back. Are you sure you don't want to join, Jemina?"

Jemina shook her head. "Nah, I don't want to spook Wanda. Besides, I saw a pair of jeans that caught my eye, and I think I might stick around a bit longer."

"Let me know if you get anything else out of Bianca," Mari whispered.

"I will."

## CHAPTER EIGHT

Mari arrived home ten minutes late. She rushed to her apartment and found, to her relief and surprise, that Wanda wasn't standing outside in the hall waiting. Figuring she must still be getting ready, Mari hurried and set the table. On the way home she had stopped at Lito Bueno's Mexican Restaurant and picked up cheese enchiladas, beef and chicken tacos, and rice and beans. The food was still steaming and her mouth watered in anticipation as she laid the plates out and rummaged through the kitchen drawer for silverware. This done, she sat down at the table and waited while Tabasco sat next to her begging for scraps.

Another ten minutes had passed, and Mari thought about going over and knocking on Wanda's door when she heard a sharp knock on her own door.

Immediately Tabasco began leaping around in circles, barking excitedly.

"Tabasco, behave," Mari scolded him as she unbolted and opened her front door.

Wanda stood there wearing an elegant floral dress and a large straw hat. She wasn't alone. At least, not entirely. In one hand she held a silver cage containing five parakeets of various sizes and colors, from lime green to tropical red.

"Mari," Wanda said as Mari ushered her into the living room. "I would like you to meet my friends." Opening the cage, Wanda introduced her birds one-by-one. "This is Pippa, this is Pickle, this one here is Bonbon, this is Tweety Pie, and this is Steve. I named Steve after my ex-husband because he picks fights with the others."

"Hi there, Steve," Mari responded, not feeling sure how to respond to this.

The sight of the birds stirred Tabasco into a frenzy. He frolicked at Wanda's feet, leaping about like a circus animal and standing up on his hind legs trying to get a better look at the birds. Wanda's birds shuffled to the back of the cage in apprehension at the sight of him.

Tabasco let out a friendly bark. Frightened, the parakeets all burst from the cage in one blinding flurry of wings. Mari, Wanda, and Tabasco gaped in surprise as they hovered, stationary, above the living room.

Wanda and Mari spent the next ten minutes trying to collect all the birds before Tabasco got hold of them, which he seemed keen to do. Standing on top of her recliner, Mari managed to catch Bonbon and Tweety Pie as they fluttered about near the blinds. Wanda slowly coaxed Pickle and Pippa onto her arm using a combination of threats and bribery.

Steve was nowhere to be seen. He was the last bird missing.

"He'll turn up, I'm sure," Wanda said. "Every now and then he'll escape into my apartment and turn up a couple of days later in the closet or shower. Just like the actual Steve, who shows up once or twice a month when he's running low on money. That's an ex for ya."

"Even though you're divorced?" Mari commented.

"Divorce still doesn't stop some people," Wanda replied in an aggrieved tone. "He still hangs around hoping I'll let take him back. I feel sorry for him at this point. He has a horrible time holding down a job. If it weren't for me, he would probably starve to death."

Mari had to admit it was very sad.

Having put away four of the five birds, they went into the kitchen and sat down to dinner. It had gotten cold in their absence. Mari tried to keep the conversation light by peppering it with humorous anecdotes about working at the family restaurant, but occasionally Wanda would interject with another story about her messy divorce.

Steve had done some pretty crazy things to get her back in his life.

Wanda's talk of Steve created a feeling of gloom over the table, and they would both sit there in silence for a minute while Mari picked at her rice and beans and tried to think of something else to say.

"Just a couple of nights ago he came over and brought me flowers," Wanda continued. "Carnations. I hate carnations. Why do those flowers even exist?"

"Who knows," Mari answered.

"I can't stand 'em," Wanda went on. "They're like the meerkats of the flower world: unsightly, unattractive, and completely useless. No one in history has found a constructive use for a carnation, nor are they ever likely to."

"So how did you react?"

"I threw them in his face, of course." Wanda shrugged and took another bite of her meal. "I told him that it would take more than a silly little bouquet to win me back."

"That'll teach him." Mari smiled politely, wondering if Wanda actually did want Steve back in her life. She talked about him enough.

"I hope you never have to meet him," Wanda said sharply. "He is a horrible man. He never takes his hat off, not even indoors. He can't cook. He can't clean. He has zero manners."

"Sounds awful," Mari said, sensing that it was probably unwise to show too much sympathy for old Steve.

At that moment Tabasco came trotting up to the table with a triumphant look. Mari's heart nearly stopped as she realized he was carrying something feathery and green in his mouth.

"Speaking of Steve," she said slowly, "I think … I think Tabasco found your missing bird."

"Steve!" Wanda cried when she caught sight of the bulldog. Tabasco set the bird down gently, and it staggered about on the tile dazed and disoriented.

"He's alive," Mari blurted out. "Oh, thank goodness."

"Why, what an excellent dog," Wanda exclaimed, stooping to pick up Steve from the floor. Tabasco beamed proudly as she patted him on the top of his head.

Mari rose and walked to the cabinet where she kept the dog treats. "He really is a good dog," she said as she handed him one. "He doesn't have a violent bone in his body. However, my dad isn't a fan."

"How could anyone not love a dog like that?" Wanda said, tickling him under the chin as he finished his treat.

"You would be surprised how many reasons my dad can find not to like something," Mari added. "Of course, it doesn't help that I usually bring him into work."

"Well, if you ever need someone to watch him during the day while you're gone," Wanda volunteered, "I would love to have him over."

Tabasco barked in agreement.

Mari found Wanda amiable enough, but she felt relieved when Wanda finally went home for the night. Sometimes she found herself missing her old life which consisted of many nights spent in the city. But she liked being home even though there were moments when she wondered what life would be like without the family restaurant.

Perhaps, there would come a day when the restaurant wouldn't need her anymore.

# CHAPTER NINE

The next morning Mari awoke to find a patch of morning sunlight streaming onto her pillow. She poured herself a cup of coffee and reached the Ham & Please deli just as it was opening. She had just enough time to question Carlos before she was needed at the restaurant.

"Welcome to Ham & Please, what can I get you?" Carlos asked as she walked in. Mari paused for a moment, but Carlos acted as if he didn't recognize her.

"Give me a second," Mari replied, scanning the menu on the wall behind the counter. As Carlos began setting out fresh bread loaves she took a quick look at the front counter. Having determined that they were alone, she said in a low voice, "So, when's the funeral?"

"I wouldn't know anything about that," Carlos responded. "I'm not in charge of planning it." The tone of his voice suggested that he wasn't particularly interested in finding out.

"Would you happen to know who *is* planning it?" Mari asked. It had never occurred to her to wonder how a person got buried if they had no friends or family to do it for them.

"I don't," Carlos answered with a dismissive wave. "Sorry. Are you going to order anything?"

"Yeah, I'll have one of your breakfast sandwiches." As she handed him cash, she added, "I was just talking to Bianca, and she seemed to think that Aimée was going through some personal things. Would you know anything about that?"

"No. Sorry."

"Really?" Mari replied, trying hard not to sound too insensitive. But Carlos was not acting like himself either. "I find that awfully hard to believe, given that you were going out with her. By all accounts you were inseparable. If there was something going on, you can tell me."

"Why?" Carlos asked.

Mari hardly believed her ears. "Your girlfriend was just murdered," she said slowly. "And if you have any information that can shed light on the last few weeks of her life, it could help with the investigation. Unless you have something to hide?"

Mari was glad she had chosen to come early and that there was no one else in the deli because the conversation was rapidly escalating.

"Me?" Carlos responded, raising his voice. "Well, last I checked, you're not on the police force. You're not a trained law enforcement officer, and I have better things to do with my time then stand here answering your ridiculous questions. If you want to play cop, go do it with someone else."

"Yes, I can see that you're awfully busy," Mari stated, looking around at the empty deli.

"If you're not out of here in ten seconds," Carlos began, "I'm calling the police."

"Carlos," Mari muttered. "Don't be like this, okay. I am just trying to help. A woman died in *my* apartment. I need answers just as much as the police do."

Carlos clenched his jaw. He looked as if he was trying to decide whether he should cooperate or ban Mari from the premises. The door chimed before he could decide and Mr. Chun, the owner of the Lucky Noodle, entered the deli.

"Welcome to Ham & Please, what can I get you?" Carlos asked as he forced a smile.

"Thanks, I'm still looking," Mr. Chun responded. He stood behind Mari with his hands folded, scanning the menu and seemingly oblivious to the tension in the room.

"What are you even doing here, Mr. Chun?" Mari hissed.

Mr. Chun adjusted his glasses and stared at her in bewilderment. "Well, if it isn't little Marisol Ramirez. Is it a crime to like breakfast sandwiches now?"

He went on reading through the menu while Carlos and Mari eyed each other uneasily, waiting for him to leave. When Mari had decided she couldn't wait anymore, she whispered, "You know where to find me."

"You're just a waitress," Carlos whispered back. "You have no business chasing down criminals. Butt out, Mari."

"You're looking guiltier by the minute," Mari said, giving up any pretense of whispering and resuming her normal voice.

Mr. Chun stared back and forth at the both of them. "I can come back later."

"No, you stay," Mari and Carlos shouted in unison. Mr. Chun looked petrified and didn't say another word.

Mari turned again to face Carlos, who looked like he wanted to smash something over her head. "Listen," she said. "Either Aimée got herself mixed up in something, or someone out there wants one of us dead. *Anyone* at my party could have been a target. Even you."

"Just get out of here," Carlos yelled.

"But, Carlos—"

"Just leave!" Carlos smacked the counter so suddenly that Mari's eyes went wide. Carlos threw off his apron. "I need to get out of here!"

Carlos stormed out of the deli leaving Mari with even more questions.

"So, does this mean I'm not getting my breakfast?" Mr. Chun asked.

## CHAPTER TEN

Mari spent her morning shift at Lito Bueno's Mexican Restaurant pondering what she knew about the case in light of her exchange with Carlos. After the party, she had almost ruled him out as a suspect because it had been hard to imagine him ever committing a murder. But now she had to reassess everything she'd thought she had known about him. Carlos had a beastly temper, and that worried her.

On the other hand, the grief could be getting to him. Aimée appeared to have been poisoned with the queso dip that Austin had brought. Her murder had been a premeditated act. Whoever killed her had done it with careful planning. Carlos's temper might not have entered into it.

Mari had never paid any particular attention to her customers' orders, but this morning it seemed like every third person ordered queso.

"Am I going mad," she asked Alex, "or does it seem like there's a lot more queso being ordered than usual?"

"Madness is always a possibility," Alex said. "On the other hand, you could be suffering from confirmation bias."

"What's that?" Mari asked.

"It's this very normal human tendency to notice things that align with our perceptions and ignore things that don't. For example, have you ever noticed that your phone buzzes right as you're getting in the shower?"

"Alex, what are you talking about?"

"Why does everyone look at me funny when I say that?" Alex replied.

"Alex, you're not helping," Mari said as she moved toward the door. "Hey, speaking of which, have you noticed that the rice and beans portions have been looking smaller?"

"Actually, yes," Alex answered. "It's another one of Dad's money saving schemes."

Mari rolled her eyes. "I told him not to do that. Customers are going to start complaining. Why does no one listen to me?"

Once her shift had ended, Mari confronted her father in his office and tried to convince him that lowering portion sizes was a terrible idea. Mari knew that portion size was a big reason they got so many customers. It came as something of a relief to both parties when David walked in and informed Mari that Jemina was working late at Woofle's and had just ordered takeout for herself and a few of her co-workers.

"I figured you would want to deliver it," David said.

"Sure, I'll go," Mari responded. She had been planning to call Jemina later anyway and tell her about the spat with Carlos.

"And take that dog with you," Mr. Ramirez added with an annoyed look on his face.

Mari grabbed Tabasco's leash and led him down the hallway and out the back door. He yelped in joyous anticipation the whole way there, sensing where they were headed and knowing that an endless supply of snacks awaited him at the end of the journey.

Mari entered the main office building belonging to Woofle's Snack Company, a business that specialized in maple-bacon dog treats. Their signature treats were shaped like waffles. Mari had always found it ironic that Jemina had secured a job there because she wasn't an animal lover.

Mari saw Austin Murphy in the break room and hurriedly carried the food toward him.

"Hello," she greeted him. "I need someone to sign this delivery form.

"Oh, it's you," Austin said, looking her up and down. "I wanted to apologize again for how things ended the other night." He fixed her with an unblinking stare that made Mari feel nervous and awkward.

"Don't apologize unless you are hiding something," she teased.

Austin laughed and laid his hand on her arm. "No, but I do feel partially responsible." Mari pulled her arm away. "I hope the police get to the bottom of this horrible event so we can all move on with our lives."

"Well, if it wasn't your food that killed Aimée then what did?" Mari asked." If there was one thing that crime-solving had taught her, it's that there *was* no murderer-type. Anyone could become a killer given the right circumstances.

The door opened, and a woman entered the break room carrying a large shopping bag. She had dark red hair the exact color of her lipstick and was wearing a homely looking sweater that reminded her of Wanda's apartment. It was rare to see anyone dressed so warm, and Mari allowed her eyes to rest on the sight as she strode towards them.

"Hey, babe," Austin commented. "You look awfully nice in that little getup. Are we going clubbing later?"

Mari rolled her eyes. Was he like this with *every* woman?

"It's not a crime to dress nice, is it?"

"If it is," Austin said softly, "then lock me up." He kissed her on the forehead as she leaned into him. Mari nodded in comprehension.

Of course.

She had always assumed he was single because of the way in which he flirted with just about every woman he saw.

"What did you bring me?"

"Well, I *did* bring you fried chicken, cauliflower, and mashed potatoes." Gesturing at the Lito Bueno's bag resting on the table behind him, she said in a disappointed tone, "I didn't know someone had already brought you dinner."

Mari decided this was as good a time as ever to intervene. "Hi. Sorry." She extended her hand. "What's your name?"

"Brenda," the woman replied. "Brenda *Murphy*. I'm Austin's wife."

"I work at Lito Bueno's Mexican Restaurant," Mari said. "A friend of mine ordered some food for herself and some coworkers. I just thought I would bring it by."

She hoped Brenda could read the subtext buried in her explanation. Mari had no intention of flirting with her husband.

"Thanks so much for that," Brenda responded, giving her a once-over. Mari couldn't tell whether or not she was being sarcastic. Turning back to Austin, she said,

"Now you have even more food if you want it."

"You know all I want is you, Brenda," Austin replied, and he pulled her in for a second kiss. Brenda smiled but said nothing.

## CHAPTER ELEVEN

Mari and Jemina shared dinner in her office which consisted of fajitas topped with guacamole, and double portions of rice and beans. Once they were settled and eating Mari told her about the exchange with Austin and Brenda.

"I can't believe how much nicer she is than Austin," Mari commented. "It always amazes me how the dumbest guys end up with these amazing women."

"He really doesn't deserve her," Jemina said sadly as she pulled the lid off her soda with a loud snap. "It took me months to realize that Austin was married."

"I would never have guessed," Mari said a little too loudly, forgetting that her voice could easily be carried through the walls. "Sorry," she said in a whisper, "it's just that he has been flirting with me nonstop since the day we met. He was even hitting on me at the party as the paramedics carried Aimée out in a body bag."

"Trust me, I know all about it," Jemina said. "He used to hit on me like crazy when I first started. He's actually calmed down a little since Dale died, probably because he didn't want to be sued for sexual harassment." Dale, Jemina's previous boss, had also been a notorious womanizer.

"How did you react?" Mari asked.

"I laid down the law," Jemina answered. "I invited his wife to play bunco.'"

"And that worked?"

"Yep," Jemina responded with a note of pride in her voice. "He slowed down after that. He was probably afraid of me telling his wife a thing or two about his extracurriculars."

"Genius," Mari said, and they both laughed.

***

Mari lingered around Jemina's office for another half-hour, recounting her argument with Carlos that morning and relaying her suspicion that he might be the murderer. They discussed it for some time. Jemina felt sure there must be some important clue that they were overlooking. But finally, Jemina was forced to throw Mari out so she could finish working. Mari returned home, where she fed Tabasco and spent the rest of the night on the couch sipping earl grey and mindlessly watching the TV.

The next morning, shortly after the restaurant opened, Rick stopped by in his policeman's uniform to pick up an order of breakfast burritos.

"Have you spoken to Jemina this morning?" he asked as he hoarded several dozen packs of hot sauce.

Mari shook her head. "I saw she had left me a voice mail just as I was pulling in, but I haven't had time to check it."

"You might want to call her," Rick replied. "She's in the hospital."

Mari set down the tray she was carrying. "Is she okay? What happened?"

"Yeah, apparently she got attacked last night. She was leaving the office to go home. It was dark, and she couldn't see who it was, but someone came up behind her and hit her on the back of the head. She's lucky she wasn't killed."

"Who found her?" Mari asked.

"One of the cleaning crew," Rick said. "They were leaving to go home when they saw a body sprawled out in the middle of the parking lot. Of course, their first assumption was that someone had been killed, so they called the police."

"Poor Jemina," Mari mumbled.

This wasn't the first time Jemina had been hurt in the course of a murder investigation. A few months earlier she had landed in the hospital after someone smashed into her car in the hopes of pushing her off the road. As she had done before, Mari convinced Alex to cover her shift and left work at once. She found Jemina lying in a hospital bed in a sparsely decorated room.

"I brought you some flowers," Mari said in an apologetic tone. "Apparently, they're out of season, and these carnations were all I could find."

"They're perfect," Jemina replied, taking them into her arms and setting them down on the nightstand. Mari let out a sigh of relief.

"So," she asked, taking a seat, "what happened? Rick said you were attacked."

"Right after you left, Austin came into my office." Jemina shuddered. "He hasn't come onto me like that since I first chewed him out. Last night, for whatever reason, he was up to his old tricks. He kept telling me how beautiful I was and ignoring my repeated hints that he needed to leave because I had work to do."

"Now I'm sorry I left," Mari responded.

"I'm sorry I threw you out," Jemina added. "Austin is not normally like that. Eventually, I realized I wasn't going to get any more work done with him hovering around, so I packed up and left."

"Recently, one of the lights went out in the parking lot, and I had to use my phone to find my car in the dark. I had this feeling like I was being watched. I felt the hairs standing up on the back of my arm, and I felt weirdly cold all over. It was like in a dream when you're running to the end of a hallway, but the end of the hallway keeps getting further and further away. No matter how fast I ran, it wasn't fast enough."

So, what happened?" Mari asked, trying to keep Jemina on track.

"I got to my car, and I was digging through my purse for my keys," Jemina explained. "The next thing I knew, I woke up at the hospital. I don't remember how I got here. All I know is that my head hurts. They told me I have a concussion."

"You were found by the cleaning crew," Mari informed her. "Who knows what would have happened if they hadn't shown up when they did."

"So, do you think it was Austin?" Jemina asked, her pulse quickening.

"I don't know what else to tell you," Mari replied. "He has a problem, and you rejected him last night. Maybe he snapped."

"Mari, help me," Jemina said. For the first time since Mari could remember, she sounded scared. "I don't want to go back to work."

# CHAPTER TWELVE

"We still haven't come to a consensus about Carlos," Mari stated.

Mari and Jemina were still sitting together in the hospital. Mari had been reading to Jemina for the last hour, but when she saw Jemina beginning to nod off, she put the book away and began brainstorming.

"Can't a girl get some sleep around here?" Jemina muttered, sitting up again. She winced in pain and clutched the back of her head. "Carlos's temper is certainly alarming, and he doesn't seem as torn up about losing his girlfriend as I thought he would be."

"That makes two suspects," Mari commented. "But what are their motives?"

"I don't know," Jemina replied. "It would help if we knew more about the nature of Carlos's relationship with Aimée. And then there's Austin who doesn't like talking about his marriage at all."

"Yeah," Mari agreed. "I wish we had some truth serum or something."

"That would be useful," Jemina responded. "Too bad we don't live in a fairytale. But on the other hand, I wouldn't want just anyone to know my deepest darkest secrets."

"My life is pretty boring," Mari replied. "My *secrets* would put people to sleep."

Jemina laughed as she rubbed the back of her head again. "Mari Ramirez," she said, "if there's one thing your life is *not*, it is boring."

"Says the one in the hospital bed," Mari reminded her.

***

As it happened, Mari didn't need truth serum. When she came into work the next morning, Carlos was seated in a corner booth studiously examining the menu. Mari gulped, wondering if he planned on causing a scene.

Mari paused in surprise when she saw him. The only other person in the building at that moment was Alex, and she would need him to keep an eye out in case Carlos lost it.

Mari still didn't know if Carlos had been the one who'd attacked Jemina in the parking lot. So far, he'd refused to explain himself. Mari texted her brother Alex to keep an eye on Carlos, and then she cautiously approached his table.

"Don't worry," he said immediately. "I'm not going to flip out on you. I just want to talk about the other day."

"I have a few minutes," Mari replied.

"I've been thinking a lot about what you said, and I want to apologize for letting my temper get the better of me," Carlos stated. "I just want Aimée to rest in peace. That is all I want."

"Okay." Mari took a deep breath and waited for more information.

"I didn't kill her." Carlos nodded. "I'm sure you think I did after our little fight, but I didn't. And I want to help you figure out who did."

"So, what do you know?"

Carlos cleared his throat. "Well, for one thing," he said with a pained look in his eyes, "you were right. Aimée had been acting differently before she died. I confronted her about it, but all she did was argue with me."

"So she never confided in you?" Mari asked.

Carlos shook his head. "No, but she didn't have to."

"What do you mean?" Mari narrowed her eyes.

Carlos anxiously glanced around before whispering, "I think she was cheating on me."

"Have you told this to the police?" Mari's eyes went wide. "This would help their investigation immensely."

"No," Carlos replied.

"Why not?"

"Because it's humiliating," Carlos blurted out a little too loudly.

"Of course," Mari said quietly. "I understand."

"That night when I left your party, I decided to move forward and never think or speak about it again. A fresh start." Carlos glanced down at the table.

"And then I came along asking too many questions," Mari added. "I get it. I didn't mean to cause you any more pain."

Carlos shook his head. "I've realized that I need to face the facts sooner or later. That is the only way I can truly move on with my life. And before you ask, the answer is no. No, I do not know who she was seeing behind my back."

"Well, I doubt her secret will stay hidden for long," Mari said, hoping she was right. "How long do you think she was cheating?"

"I don't know," he replied. "We had just had another one of our arguments the night of your party. She didn't speak to me at all and then ... she was gone."

"What were you fighting about, if you don't mind me asking?" Mari asked.

"That's just the thing," Carlos replied. Mari could tell that he had been holding this in for a while. The more he talked, the easier the words came out. "I don't know. She was texting someone before we left for your place. I asked her who it was and she went off on some rant about how I never give her any space."

"Interesting." Mari scratched her chin. "If only we had her cell phone."

"I think she planned on meeting her lover that night after the party." Carlos shook his head. "Man, it does feel good to get this off of my chest."

"What makes you say that?"

"Because I wanted her to come home with me, but she said she had plans," he explained. "I asked her what she was planning on doing, and she went on another rant."

"So, if we can figure out who she was texting that night, we might get some more answers." Mari thought through the night of her housewarming party for the hundredth time. She was sure that the answer was right under her nose.

## CHAPTER THIRTEEN

After Carlos had left the restaurant, Mari sat in his booth for some time sifting through all the clues. Ever since the attack on Jemina, a thought had been tugging at the back of her mind. What if she and the police had been looking in the wrong places this whole time? Maybe the intended victim hadn't been Aimée at all, but Jemina. That would have explained why she had been attacked in the parking lot, though if that was the case, it was remarkable how clumsy and the murderer had been. He or she had poisoned the queso dip that anyone could have eaten, killing the wrong person, and hadn't even managed to kill Jemina before the night crew found her.

Either that or Jemina was just remarkably lucky.

Despite the fact that Austin appeared to have been the attacker, she still hadn't ruled out the possibility that Carlos had been the murderer. Despite his avowed determination to find the real killer, it was clear that his relationship with the victim had been troubled. Mari had a sneaking suspicion that his account of the fight they had had just before the party had omitted some key details. She had seen how worked up Carlos could get, and she didn't doubt he'd said or done things in the heat of the moment that he wouldn't dare admit.

On the other hand, there was a third party whom they hadn't much taken into account yet, and that was the man Aimée had seen in secret. Perhaps she had been lying to him just as she had been lying to Carlos. Maybe that man had learned she was already in a relationship, or that she was cheating on both him and Carlos. Perhaps this mystery man had killed her?

Mari had hoped that Carlos's visit would be the last surprise of her morning, so it was disappointing and a little aggravating when Austin Murphy showed up at Lito Bueno's for lunch. All the more so when he insisted on being seated in Mari's corner of the restaurant.

"So we meet again," Austin said when he saw her. "I think I'll start with an appetizer. How about some of those egg rolls with sweet and sour sauce?"

"I think you wandered into the wrong restaurant," Mari commented. "You'll be wanting the Lucky Noodle across the street."

"Any restaurant is the right restaurant if you're there," he replied. He folded the menu with an impish grin and handed it back to her. "I'll have some water."

"Are you going to order any food?" Mari asked.

"Now that you mention it, I am feeling pretty hungry," Austin replied. He paused for a second before adding, "Hungry for some lovin'."

"Alright, I've had enough," Mari said, turning on her heels and storming into the kitchen.

The kitchen was empty. Mari glanced at the time and realized that it was the middle of the shift change. She found the nearest phone and began dialing the number of the police station. She slammed the phone down after she realized that she didn't know what to say. Austin was sleazy, but she had nothing to report.

Mari swore in frustration, wondering how a man like that got away with such behavior. It sickened her. She was glad she didn't work in the same office as Austin like Jemina did.

The door to the kitchen swung open. Mari glanced up in relief, hoping it might be one of her brothers, but it wasn't.

It was Austin.

"Hey, I never got my water," Austin said boldly. "I just wanted to make sure nothing had happened to you."

Mari inched toward a drawer where the knives were kept. Austin didn't seem to notice. "Stay back," she said in a threatening voice. "I know what you did to Jemina."

"I don't know what you're talking about," Austin replied. "To be honest, I was hoping you might be able to tell me where she is. She hasn't been at work all day, and I was getting worried. I know the two of you are close. Close enough for a wild night of self-exploration, I wonder?"

"Ewww," Mari said as Austin moved closer to her. "You're married, remember?"

"That hasn't stopped me before," he answered. "And I've seen the way you look at me."

"That look is called *disdain*," Mari commented. "Honestly, do you think every woman you meet wants to sleep with you or something? Who would even go for that?"

"I like 'em feisty." Austin appeared to be completely ignorant of Mari's body language. To Mari's horror, he leaned in for a kiss. She shoved him, and he went stumbling backward into the pot rack, sending pots flying all over the kitchen with a deafening clamor. At the same instant, the kitchen door flew open and Alex and David came running in.

"What is he doing in here?" Alex asked.

"Get him out of here," Mari demanded.

"Looks like someone won't be finishing his meal," David commented as he and his brother circled Austin. "Shame."

"I'm afraid we have a strict *no losers* policy, sir," Alex chimed in.

Both of Mari's brothers were considerably larger than Austin, and he squeaked in alarm as they pulled him off of the floor and began pushing him toward the door.

"Easy there, son," Austin complained. "These suits don't come cheap."

"Don't tempt me," David replied.

"Don't come back here," said Mari firmly said. "Ever."

"Playing hard to get already," Austin responded.

"This isn't a game," Mari argued. She stopped suddenly, hitting her forehead with the palm of her hand. She couldn't believe she hadn't seen it before. "Or maybe it was?"

"Excuse me?" Austin answered, confused by her change of tone.

"That's it." Mari shook her head. "It really *was* you, wasn't it? You killed Aimée Carver."

"What?" Austin's expression changed completely.

"Yes, you chased after her, but she kept on rejecting you." Mari cleared her throat. "So, you killed her."

"Yikes," Alex added. "I think you took it a little too far this time, bro."

"But I didn't," Austin argued. "I didn't kill her." A bead of sweat dripped down his brow.

"You did," Mari insisted. "And that's exactly what I'm going to tell Detective Price."

"I didn't kill her," Austin shouted. "I *loved* her!"

## CHAPTER FOURTEEN

The moment Austin was gone, Mari retrieved her cell phone and called Rick.

"You're not going to believe this," she said. "Austin Murphy just came into the restaurant. He tried to kiss me."

"What?" Rick exclaimed on the other end of the line. "I hope you decked him for that."

"Alex and David took care of him," Mari reassured him. "But that's not all. He told me that he was in love with Aimée. They were having a secret affair."

"He told you that?"

"Yeah," Mari replied. "Who would have guessed, right?"

"That still doesn't mean he's not a killer," Rick said. "Plenty of people kill for love. Be careful, Mari. Don't let him hang around you anymore. He could be dangerous."

"So, you still think he could've attacked Jemina?"

"Mari, he was the only one there that night," Rick responded. "In fact, maybe he did it because he thought Jemina knew about the affair. That means he could be back for you as well."

"Given the way he's been acting," Mari added, "I think you might be right."

Rick was silent for a minute. "There has already been too much death around here. I don't know what I would do if something happened to you too."

"Don't worry, Officer," Mari said playfully. "I can handle myself."

"Yes." Rick chuckled. "Yes, I know you can."

\*\*\*

The rest of the day dragged by for Mari. Outside the sun was slowly setting, bathing the dining room of Lito Bueno's Mexican Restaurant in hues of red and gold. Mari ate a quick dinner and worked through the dinner rush, trying not to think about Carlos and Austin and the thousands of other issues that were demanding her attention. She was anxious to be done with her shift so she could run by the hospital again to see Jemina.

The crowd in the restaurant thinned out, and Mari swept the back rooms in preparation for closing when she noticed a curious thing. Someone had left the back door open.

Seeing this, her pulse raced. She remembered the last time the back door had been left open and what that had followed. It hadn't been good. She ran to close it, and then took a deep breath to calm herself down.

"It's okay, Mari," she said aloud. "It doesn't mean anyone is after you. Those are all just memories now."

She edged slowly into the back office where she found Alex changing the coffee filter.

"Hi," she said, "did you leave the back door open?"

Alex shook his head. "No, why?" He looked up and saw the distressed look on her face. "I'm sure it's probably nothing. Sometimes David leaves it open when he's airing the rugs out."

In all the years she had been working there, Mari couldn't remember David ever doing that. "I didn't see him," she said.

"He probably left already," Alex said. "And so should you. We're closed. You don't need to be here anymore. Do you need a ride?"

She shook her head. "I'm headed over to the hospital just as soon as I find Tabasco."

"He was under that table a few minutes ago," Alex commented. "Maybe Dad finally had enough of him and chucked him outside."

Mari began to regret not accepting his offer for a ride home as she walked through the restaurant calling out Tabasco's name. She heard the doors clicking shut as Alex and the rest of the staff left for the night, and she was left alone in the restaurant. Through the dining room windows, she saw Mr. Chun standing outside the Lucky Noodle closing up for the night also. The light of a lonely street lamp cast a dim glow over the nearly empty street.

"Tabasco?" Mari called out. "Tabasco, it's time to go home. Where are you?"

But Tabasco wasn't lurking in any of his usual hiding spots. She didn't find him hiding under the tables in the dining room, and he wasn't curled up behind the potted plant in the entrance hall, and he wasn't resting under the long Spanish-style bench by the front door.

Annoyed and a little worried, she called David to ask if he had seen him. But David's phone went straight to voicemail. She remembered him saying he would be going out after work with his girlfriend. She shook her head and hung up the phone.

There weren't many places left to look, but she decided to check the office one more time. Tabasco wasn't in there. But as she was coming out into the hallway, she heard something that sent chills down her spine. The sound of quiet scuffling and muffled voices.

Unnerved, Mari crept closer to the kitchen door. She was sure everyone else had gone home for the night. Just as she leaned her head against it, a pot came crashing to the floor on the other side, and she shrieked.

Someone was in the kitchen, and she was going to find out who it was. With her phone in her hand, she pushed open the door.

A man stood by the stove with his back against the window. His collared shirt crisply ironed slacks, and dark wavy hair was unmistakable.

It was Austin Murphy.

He was back.

## CHAPTER FIFTEEN

"Austin?" Mari said, stepping into the kitchen. The harsh glare of the fluorescent lights hurt her eyes, making it hard to see. "Why are you tied up like that?"

Austin said something she couldn't understand. As she cautiously approached him, she saw that his mouth had been gagged by a thick layer of duct tape. Her heart quickened as she realized the obvious. Austin wasn't the only person in the room. Someone else had tied him up.

"Who did this to you?" she asked as she reached for the tape.

But Austin let out a muffled cry as he shook his body in hopes of escaping. Every hair on the back of Mari's neck rose on end as she backed away toward the door, never taking her eyes off of him for a moment.

Her body went limp as she backed into Austin's tormentor.

It was Brenda Murphy.

"Hello, Mari," she said in a faux-courteous voice. "Fancy meeting you here."

Her red hair hung wildly across her face, and a deranged look came into her eyes as she lifted a shiny metal object. She pressed the cold steel of a gun against the back of Mari's neck.

"Sit down," Brenda said, motioning toward a chair that stood against the back wall. When Mari didn't move quickly enough, Brenda shoved her. "I said, sit down!"

Mari's hands shook as she took a seat beside Austin. "Brenda," she said in as steady a voice as she could muster, "why are you doing this? Why—why did you tie up Austin?"

"Because he's a horrible man," Brenda said in a voice of unnerving calm, "and he deserves to die."

The words fell like a hammer, shattering Mari's assumptions into small pieces. It occurred to her that she might have been wrong about Austin this whole time. Perhaps he hadn't been the one to poison his own queso dip.

"I just want to know one thing," Mari said. "Did you kill Aimée Carver because she and Austin were having an affair?"

To Mari's surprise, Brenda smiled. It was almost as though she was grateful to have been found out. "When I read through the messages on Austin's phone," Brenda admitted, "and found out he was seeing her, I went to the boutique and confronted Aimée in person. I wanted to let her know, in case she didn't already, that the man she was seeing was married. I told her who I was, but she laughed in my face."

"I'm sorry," Mari said, hoping that sympathy might save her.

"Before I met Aimée, I thought it might have been some innocent mistake on her part," Brenda continued. "Not on his, of course." She waved the gun at Austin, whose eyes were red and tear-streaked. "He knew exactly what he was doing. But it turned out that Aimée knew we were married and she had no intention of breaking it off. Since trying to reason with her had failed, I decided that more drastic measures had to be taken."

"The poison." Mari gulped. "You were the one who poisoned her."

Brenda nodded proudly. "No one ever thought to ask Austin who made his little queso dip. One night when Austin thought he was alone in the house, I overheard them talking on the phone. She told him she'd discovered a new favorite food and that she couldn't resist eating it whenever it was put in front of her. The moment I heard that a plan began forming in my mind."

"And my housewarming party provided you with the perfect opportunity, "Mari added.

"Austin told me he was attending a party with some of his coworkers," Brenda responded, casually pointing her gun at him. "I knew that Aimée was going to be there, and my suspicions were confirmed when I asked if I could come along and Austin told me it wasn't a good idea. I made queso the morning of the party and told him to take it. The fool took it to your apartment willingly."

"You could have killed anyone, Brenda," Mari pointed out. "Your plan was deeply flawed."

"It worked," Brenda said proudly, and to Mari's horror she produced a red canister of gasoline from behind the counter. "And in a few minutes, my plan will be complete."

"Brenda," Mari responded, unable to take her eyes off the canister of gasoline, "what are you doing? Brenda, you don't have to do this. The woman you wanted to punish is already dead. I know you are upset with Austin, but murder is not the answer."

Brenda laughed a hollow laugh. "My husband is not even remotely upset. The day after his little mistress died he was up to his old tricks, brazenly flirting with that hussy he works with at the office. He will *never* quit, and he will *never* learn."

Brenda set her gun down on the counter and began moving forward, slinging the gasoline across the tiles at their feet. Mari glanced at Austin. An eerie sense of serenity seemed to have come over him as if he had resigned himself to the fact that he was about to die.

Thinking furiously, Mari realized that she would have to distract Brenda with questions if they were to have any hope of getting out of there alive. "I should have listened more closely to Bianca," she said. "Bianca mentioned that Aimée kept showing up late for work."

"It doesn't matter now," Brenda replied. "She is gone."

"*Hussy* he works with?" Mari continued, repeating Brenda's accusation from earlier. "Do you mean Jemina?"

"Don't say her name in front of me." Brenda spat. "I know they've been seeing each other also. Austin tried to spoon-feed me some garbage about having to work late at the office that night, but I saw right through it. I would have killed her, too, if the cleaning crew hadn't interrupted me."

"Jemina is not your enemy, believe me," Mari said as Brenda rummaged through drawers. "She has never laid a finger on Austin."

"Well, soon it won't matter, anyway," Brenda replied. With a look of triumph, she produced a box of matches and held it up to the light. "I'm going to blow him and everyone he ever flirted with sky-high. As soon as I'm done with you, I'll find Jemina and make her pay for the sins she's committed."

Austin let out a low whimper as Brenda reached into the box and pulled out a single match.

## CHAPTER SIXTEEN

Mari shut her eyes.

She heard the distant drone of a truck passing on the street, unaware of the flames that were about to ensue. There was no one out on the street. Mr. Chun had gone home for the night, or she might have risked yelling. Mari heard her mother's wind chimes tinkling in the spring wind.

Mari thought of her family, and how devastated they would be to find her dead and the family restaurant burned to a crisp. She had made such an effort to move farther away from them, and now she wished she was closer to them.

Mari took a deep breath. There must have been something she could say that would talk Brenda out of what she was about to do.

Something.

"You know," Mari said aloud, and she was surprised to hear herself say it, "I never thought I would wish to hear the sound of my father's voice one last time. It's funny the way life turns out."

"Stop talking, please," said Brenda replied. "You're making this harder than it needs to be."

It was a curious admission for Brenda to make. Mari decided to keep talking. "I remember going out to Tortoise Lake when I was little, and dipping my feet in the water. I've spent the rest of my life wishing I could be as happy as I was by that lake at the age of eight. I had no worries back then. Have you ever been to Tortoise Lake?"

"Enough," Brenda shouted, the match shaking in her hand. "Y'all deserve this. *He* deserves this!"

Mari looked to the kitchen door and smiled. Brenda had been so distracted by Mari's chatter that she hadn't paid any attention to the dog barking in the doorway, nor noticed that her gun was now in someone else's possession.

"Put the match down," Wanda said, aiming the gun at Brenda. Her hands trembled. "Do as I say or you'll be sorry."

Brenda laughed coldly. "Do you even know how to shoot that thing?" she asked. "You look like you've never held a gun in your life."

"Look," Wanda responded, every muscle in her face tight. "I know how hard it is to see the man you love running around with other women. I put up with it for twenty years, waiting for him to come home at night. I know how much it hurts and I know how tempting it is to want to set the world on fire, but it's not worth it. Believe me."

"I don't care anymore," cried Brenda. "I'm tired of being lonely. I've spent my whole life being lonely."

She ran the match along the edge of the matchbox. At the same instant, Wanda shut her eyes tightly and fired the gun. It went off with a loud bang and struck Brenda's arm. She let out a scream and fell over, moaning in pain. To Mari's relief, the match remained unlit.

***

One week later, on a calm and cloudless Sunday, Wanda came into the restaurant to eat lunch with Mari. To Mari's surprise, Mr. Ramirez had insisted on seating her personally. Then, to the surprise of everyone present, he announced that Wanda's meal was on the house.

"Let this be a lesson to all of you," he said. "If you save my restaurant from burning down, you will be richly rewarded."

"Not to mention the life of his only daughter," Mari cleverly added. "Don't forget about that."

Wanda happily ordered her usual chicken enchiladas.

"Thank you for everything," Mari said, nudging a bowl of salsa her way. "I've realized that being here with family is the most important thing I can be doing right now."

"I did all that?" Wanda responded.

"There's more to this town than I see sometimes," Mari continued. "People around here never cease to surprise me."

Wanda beamed. "Don't thank me. Thank your dog."

"Tabasco?"

"Yes," Wanda said with a laugh. "I was bringing him back that night. I found him wandering around in the parking lot outside your apartment, and I figured you were searching for him. You weren't at home which meant that you were here at the restaurant. I didn't want you to worry."

"I see," Mari replied, slipping the dog a piece of grilled chicken under the table. "Tabasco saves the day once again."

"Is your life always this exciting?" Wanda asked, wide-eyed.

"I don't know if *exciting* is the right word, Wanda."

"Well, here's to good times." Wanda raised her glass. "And more *exciting* adventures."

"I'll drink to that first part," Mari said. She and Wanda clinked their glasses together while Tabasco barked in agreement.

# BOOKS BY HOLLY PLUM

## PATTY CAKES BAKE SHOP COZY MYSTERIES
*Until Death Do Us Tart*
*For Butter Or For Worse*
*Something Bakes and Something Blue*
*Frying The Knot*
*Wedding Bells and a Body*
*Saying Pie Do*

## MEXICAN CAFÉ COZY MYSTERIES
*Murder Con Carne*
*Killer Salsa*
*Smothered In Lies*
*Rice, Beans, and Revenge*
*Crimes and Chimichangas*
*Soft Taco Murder*

Thank you for your support! If you would like to know more about new releases and other fun things, sign up for my author newsletter by visiting my author page on Amazon.com.

Printed in Great Britain
by Amazon